MARTIN COUNTY
Community Redevelopment Agency

MARTIN COUNTY BOARD OF COUNTY COMMISSIONERS

District 1 Doug Smith
District 2 Ed Fielding, Vice Chair
District 3 Ann Scott
District 4 Sarah Heard, Chair
District 5 John Haddox

MARTIN COUNTY
Community Redevelopment Agency

MARTIN COUNTY COMMUNITY REDEVELOPMENT AGENCY

District 1 Doug Smith
District 2 Ed Fielding, Vice Chair
District 3 Ann Scott
District 4 Sarah Heard, Chair
District 5 John Haddox

COMMUNITY DEVELOPMENT STAFF

Kev Freeman, Director
Edward Erfurt, Urban Designer
Nakeischea Smith, AICP, Community Development Specialist
Nancy Johnson, Community Development Specialist
Erik Ferguson, PE, Project Engineer

Dynamic   Innovative   Sustainable

GOLDEN GATE • HOBE SOUND • INDIANTOWN • JENSEN BEACH • PALM CITY • PORT SALERNO • RIO

Table of Contents

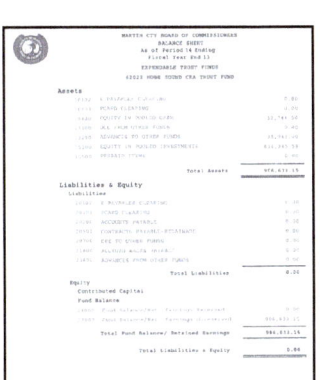

Executive Summary

CRA Successes

The Martin County Community Redevelopment Agency's (CRA) seven redevelopment areas undertook many planning and development projects in fiscal year 2013. These projects which are detailed within this annual report where conceived by the residents of the redevelopment area and adopted in the seven community redevelopment area Community Development Plans.

The CRA saw renewed interest from the private sector to invest in the redevelopment areas. In 2013, the CRA saw an increased in the number of development inquiries and building permits issues. In 2013 there was a $1.2 million dollar increase in permit valuations by the private sector within the redevelopment areas compared to the previous year. These investments are leading to a growth in the County's tax base and a growth in the Tax Increment Finance (TIF) revenue for the CRA.

Project Highlights

The 12-month period ending September 30, 2013 included various highlights throughout the Martin County Community Redevelopment Agency's seven Neighborhood Planning Areas:

CRA WIDE PROJECTS
The Community Redevelopment Agency (CRA) spearheaded several initiatives designed to benefit all seven community redevelopment areas as a whole:

- Completed the development of Google 3D maps to assist in planning and visioning for future redevelopment.
- Completed annual analysis of the per acre taxable values throughout the redevelopment areas.

- Coordinated with Martin County Departments for possible acquisition of blighted properties in the CRA.
- Provided Redevelopment Technical Assistance for properties within the redevelopment areas.
- Conducted design review and permitting for projects throughout the Planning Areas.
- Continued to draft the Community Oriented Code which will streamlined the code for redevelopment.
- Began the development of a Business Training Program to support local microentrepreneurs .

GOLDEN GATE
- The Railroad Avenue Commercial Revitalization roadway project is under construction will be completed by the end of 2013

HOBE SOUND
- Conceptual design for the Bridge Road main street completed. Final Engineering and right of way donations underway.

INDIANTOWN

- The Indiantown McDonalds/Dollar General opened greating over 80 new jobs in Indiantown.
- The site work at Carter Park is complete. Habitat for Humanity and the Boys and Girls Club have begun vertical construction.

JENSEN BEACH

- Continued design and planning activities for Indian River Drive "Complete Streets" transformation.

OLD PALM CITY

- Continued design and planning for the Mapp Road Town Center streetscape improvement project to include innovative stormwater management.

PORT SALERNO

- The Manatee Creek Micro Area Action Plan (MAP) was completed and adopted. Staff is working with the community to construction the first phase.

RIO

- New native, drought tolerant, streetscape was installed on Rhodes Avenue to transition from the commercial uses and to provide a gateway to the neighborhood.
- The Rio Porches development is pending final site plan approval. The site has been cleared of the blighted buildings, the 707 improvements are complete, and utilities will be extended south on Orange Avenue.
- The Rio Community completed the Rio Placemaking Plan which outlines the community's goals of creating a vibrant, livable community, with a strong sense of place.
- Over 75% of 707 through Rio has been resurfaced which included the sidewalk walk extensions and new bike lanes.

Introduction

The Martin County Community Redevelopment Agency (CRA) is pleased to submit the Annual Report for fiscal year ending September 30, 2013, as required by Florida Statute Section 163.356(3)(c) and Martin County Code Section 39.3.B.5.

It is the philosophy of the Community Redevelopment Agency to keep all interested parties informed with respect to the activities of the CRA and to encourage active participation in the implementation of redevelopment programs benefiting the entire community. This report enables readers to gain an understanding of CRA's operation and financial activity for fiscal year 2013.

This annual report outlines the activities and programs that the Martin County Community Redevelopment Agency managed, funded, collaborated, or supported, between October 1, 2012 and September 30, 2013. This Report also reflects cooperation and coordination in planning, redevelopment, and development activities between and among the Martin County CRA, County Departments, citizens, regional agencies, and state and federal government agencies.

We believe the data, as presented, is accurate in all material respects and that all necessary disclosures have been acknowledged.

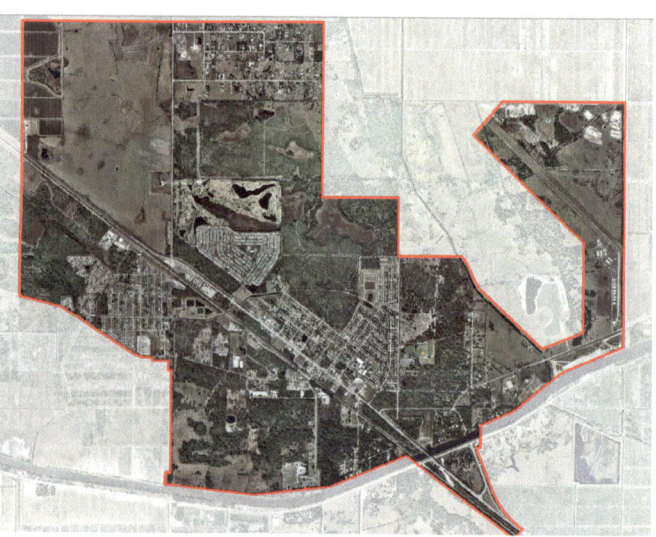

What is a CRA?

A Community Redevelopment Agency (CRA) is a public entity that finances redevelopment within focused areas. These areas tend to be older neighborhoods where there is a need to reverse deterioration, create jobs, revitalize the business climate, increase property values and encourage active participation and investment by citizens.

In order to be legally established, a Community Redevelopment Agency (CRA) must adhere to the guidelines as outlined in the Community Redevelopment Act (Chapter 163, Part III, Florida Statutes). In summary, the Act outlines the process for creating a CRA as follows:

1. Adopt the Finding of Necessity, a field study that formally identifies conditions within the established boundaries of the area.
2. Develop and adopt a Community Redevelopment Plan. The plan should address the unique needs of the targeted area and include overall goals as well as identify programs and projects
3. Establish a Redevelopment Trust Fund enabling the CRA Board to direct a percentage of property tax revenues to the target areas in order to implement the redevelopment plan.

Once established, the CRA is able to carry out redevelopment and revitalization within designated communities employing the most appropriate use of resources consistent with the public interest. Martin County has seven community redevelopment areas that the CRA oversees: Golden Gate, Hobe Sound, Indiantown, Jensen beach, Old Palm city, Port Salerno and Rio.

MARTIN COUNTY
Community Redevelopment Agency

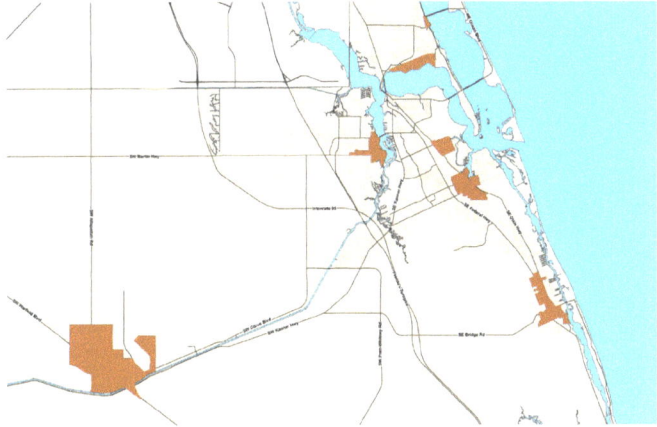

Above: *The overview map highlights the boundaries of the Community Redevelopment Areas in Martin County.*

Organizational Structure

Board of County Commissioners

The Martin County Board of County Commissioners (BOCC) is the Governing body that controls and directs the activities of the Community Redevelopment Agency. The BOCC:

- Sets the amount of TIF received by the CRA (Tax Increment Finance)
- Approves and allocates funds for redevelopment projects.
- Appoints Community Redevelopment Agency members.
- Appoints Neighborhood Advisory Committee members.

Community Redevelopment Agency

The mission of the Martin County Community Redevelopment Agency is "To promote a distinctive community identity and vibrant local economy through inclusive community engagement."
The BOCC has vested limited authority to the Community Redevelopment Agency (CRA) to carry out redevelopment and related activities within the seven designated community redevelopment areas. CRA members oversee that programs and activities are carried out as outlined in the seven Community Redevelopment Plans.

The Martin County Board of County Commissioners, as the governing body, sits as the Community Redevelopment Agency.

Neighborhood Advisory Committee

Each of the Martin County community redevelopment areas has its own Neighborhood Advisory Committee (NAC).

NAC members provide advice and recommendations to the Community Redevelopment Agency regarding the implementation of projects adopted within the Community Redevelopment Plans. This can include the proposal of amendments and modifications to the CRA Plans when needed.

To be appointed as an NAC member, an individual must be either:

1. A resident of the respective community redevelopment area, or
2. A resident of Martin County, who is also a business owner of a business located within the respective Community Redevelopment Area; or
3. A resident of Martin County, who is also a senior manager of a business located within the respective Community Redevelopment Area; or
4. A resident of Martin County, who also owns real property within a half mile of the respective Community Redevelopment Area*.

*No more than two members of any respective Neighborhood Advisory Committee will be appointed from category 4 above.

NAC Members

In FY13 the Board of County Commissioners appointed the following members of the Neighborhood Advisory Committees:

Golden Gate
Jan DalCorso - Joseph Hatton III
Mariann Moore - Althea Redway
Michael Wilchak

Hobe Sound
Mike Baker - Bruce Duncan
Angela Hoffman - Gretchen Reich
Luis Reyneri

Indiantown
Craig Bauzenberger Sr. - Donna Carman
Catherine Deninger - John (Art) Matson
Bernice Simpson

Jensen Beach
Sharon Adams - Glenda Burgess
Stephen Dutcher - Maria Lindberg
Robert McElroy - Frank Wacha Jr.

Palm City
Craig Ahal - Joseph Gilio
Jane Landrum - Douglas Legler
Thomas Plymale - Mike Searle
Tracy Seegott - Rex Sentell
Chuck Smith

Port Salerno
Ellan Asselin - Gloria Burns McHardy
Arthur Cox -Doug Delater
Cynthia Oakowsky - Edward Olsen Jr.
Catherine Winters - Karen Worden

Rio
Myra Galoci - Debra Harsh
Robert Hoza - Jim Lopilato
William Skaryd - Robert Taylor
M. Brent Waddell - David Wishart
Richard Zurich

Community Development Department

The staff of the Community Development Department acts as the liaison between the Board of County Commissioners, Community Redevelopment Agency, the Neighborhood Advisory Committees (NAC) =0and local citizens. In addition, this small team provides administrative, planning, zoning, urban design, and community outreach services to the seven community redevelopment areas.

Kevin Freeman - Director is a professional Town Planner and member of the Royal Town Planning Institute, educated in England he has worked in several communities throughout the United States over the past six years. He brings a specialty interest in sustainability and an approach that seeks to integrate sustainability with community design, transportation impact and local economic development. Prior to this position he was the Development Director at the City of Stuart Fl. and the Assistant Director of Development at Castle Rock CO. He brings significant project management experience to the table from his time as the Acquisition and Planning manager of a private consultancy working with T-Mobile in the UK. Kevin holds a Masters in Urban and Regional Planning from Sheffield Hallam University (England) and a Diploma Town Planning from Sheffield City Polytechnic

Edward Erfurt - Urban Designer is a trained architect and is currently the urban designer for the seven Neighborhood Planning Areas in Martin County, Florida. For the past seven years, he has worked around the country integrating urban design and architecture strategies for redeveloping suburban and urban environments that reflect the need to build walkable communities. Edward has developed Pattern Books and Community Vision Books across the country that promote cities, towns, and neighborhoods, which are beautiful and of lasting value. This body of work builds on the unique character that makes the tapestry of place. He holds a Master of Architectural Design and Urbanism from the University of Notre Dame, and a Bachelor of Architecture from the University of Miami.

Nakeischea Smith - Community Development Specialist is a professional planner and certified by the American Institute of Certified Planners. Originally from the Bahamas, she spent several years on staff with the Government of the Bahamas Public Works Department. There she was involved in the creation of several long range plans for islands throughout The Bahamas in addition to serving as a reviewer for large scale resort development projects. She also spearheaded efforts to relocate the container shipping port in downtown Nassau to make way for redevelopment and revitalization of the historic business district. Nakeischea applies her redevelopment knowledge and experience to revitalization efforts within Martin County's seven community redevelopment areas. A firm believer in bottom up planning, she enjoys interacting with business owners and residents throughout the community redevelopment areas and helping them achieve their community vision. Nakeischea is a proud alumni of both the Massachusetts Institute of Technology and Northeastern Illinois University where she holds a Master of City Planning and Bachelor of Arts in Sociology respectively.

Nancy Johnson, Community Development Specialist is a Colombian native with international experience in the collection and analysis of market research and strategic planning. Nancy, in addition to her experience in the USA, has worked in South America, and Europe. This experience specialized in the development of marketing plans to maximize market opportunities and contribute to company promotion and growth. Nancy holds a Masters in Marketing and Market Research with specialty in Marketing Communication from the Universidad de Valencia in Valencia, Spain, and a Bachelor in Business Administration from the Universidad del Norte in Barranquilla, Colombia.

Erik Ferguson - Project Engineer is a professional engineer with over 16 years of engineering experience. His work experience ranges from designing major highway and bridge projects for both the New York and North Carolina Department of Transportation, to administration of the Dutchess County Public Works Department in Poughkeepsie, NY. For the past six years Erik has worked as a project engineer with Martin County focusing on traffic signal, traffic calming and intersection improvements. Erik brings an interest in cost effectively creating a sustainable transportation system. Erik holds a Bachelor of Science in Civil Engineering from the University at Buffalo.

Funding Sources

General Funds

The CRA teams with County Departments on many projects throughout the community redevelopment areas. This allows the agency to maximize available Tax Increment Financing (TIF) funds and results in enhanced projects. Contributions by Commissioners utilizing designated district funds also helps in the implementation of projects.

Grants

Community Development Department Staff continuously identifies and pursue appropriate funding opportunities within state, federal, and local agencies to support CRA initiatives. Staff has worked diligently to complete grant applications, gather necessary documents or data, and prepare reports as necessary.

The CRA also liaise with County departments, private partners, and non-profits to synthesize competitive application packets, submit grant applications in a timely manner, and monitor results.

Private Investment

The private sector investment in the community redevelopment areas can be measured through the number and valuation of building permits. Since the adoption of the seven Community Redevelopment Areas, over $320 million in building and site improvements have been invested in those areas. These investments contribute to the implementation of the community vision and are reflected in the growth of the Tax Increment Finance (TIF).

In 2013, 935 residential and commercial building permits were issued within the boundaries of the CRA, accounting for 9% of the total building permits for unincorporated Martin County. These permits totaled $12,409,997.20 in private investment which is a $1.2 million increase from 2012. These permits result in construction, which provides visual evidence of improvement. This private investment will be reflective in next year's property valuations.

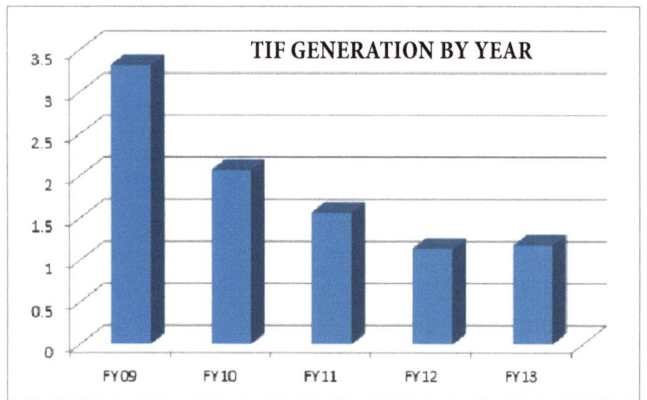

Tax Increment Financing or TIF

The Martin County Community Redevelopment Agency's activities and staff are primarily funded through Tax Increment Financing or TIF.

TIF is a mechanism which captures a percentage of any new tax revenue generated when a vacant or underutilized property is redeveloped. The base year for tax revenue is set as the year in which the community redevelopment area was established. As the majority of redevelopment areas within Martin County were established between 2000 and 2001, the CRA receives a percentage of any tax revenues greater than the amount of revenue captured in those base years. This percentage can range between 50% and 95%. In fiscal year 2013, the Board of County Commissioners allocated 75% of this increase as TIF funds to be used in the community redevelopment areas.

Generating TIF does not require an additional tax levy or a supplementary assessment on property owners. It is not an additional tax. TIF is one of the tools available to Martin County to leverage funds to promote private sector investment within the primary urban service boundary, and to generate revenues to finance projects.

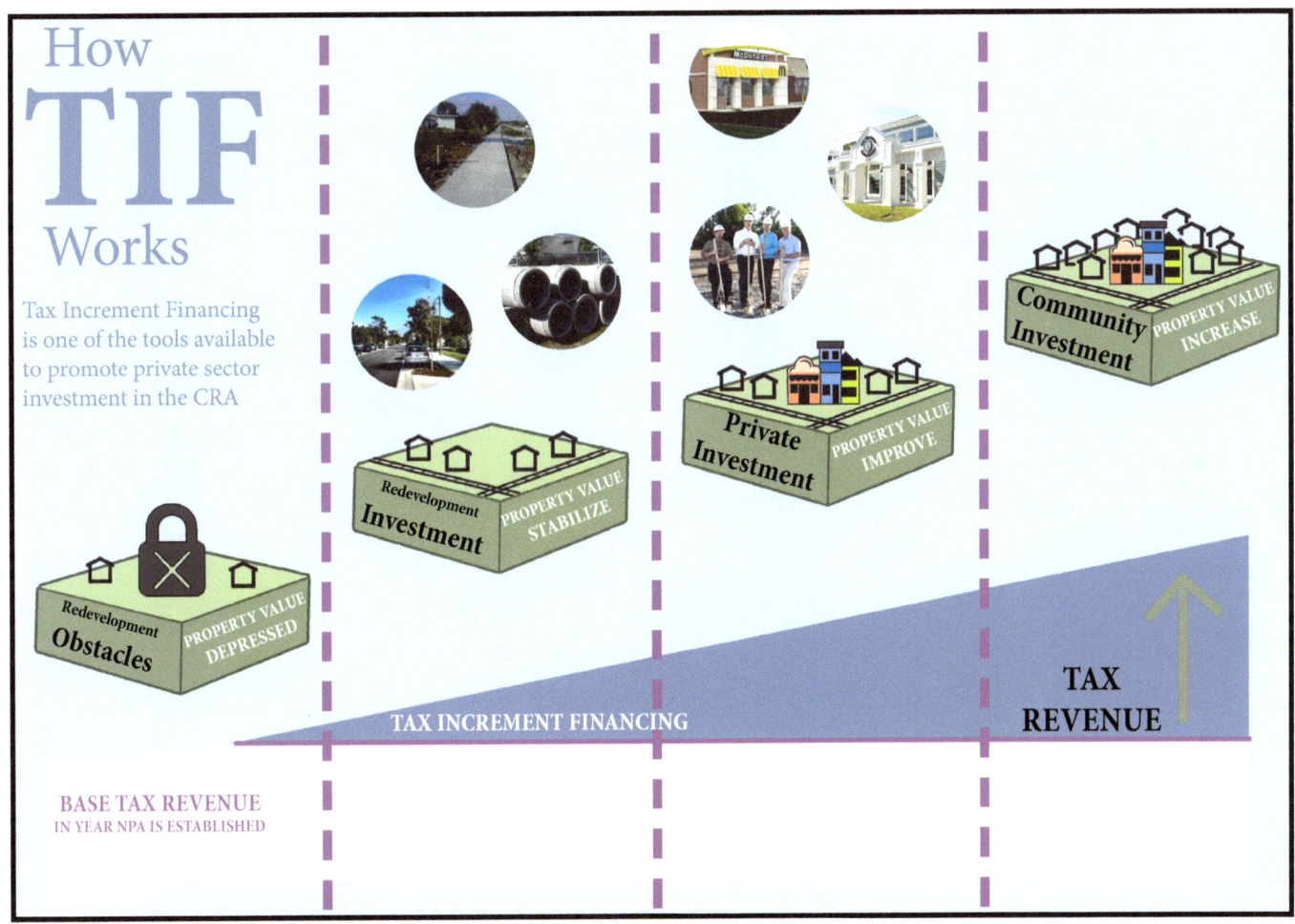

Martin County Board of County Commissioners
Your County, Your Community

CRA Wide Projects

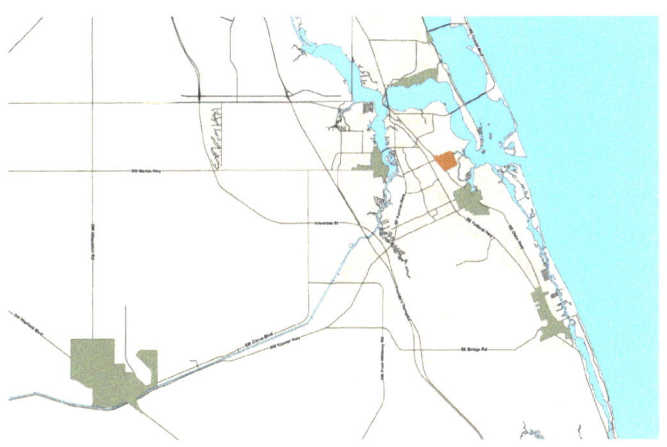

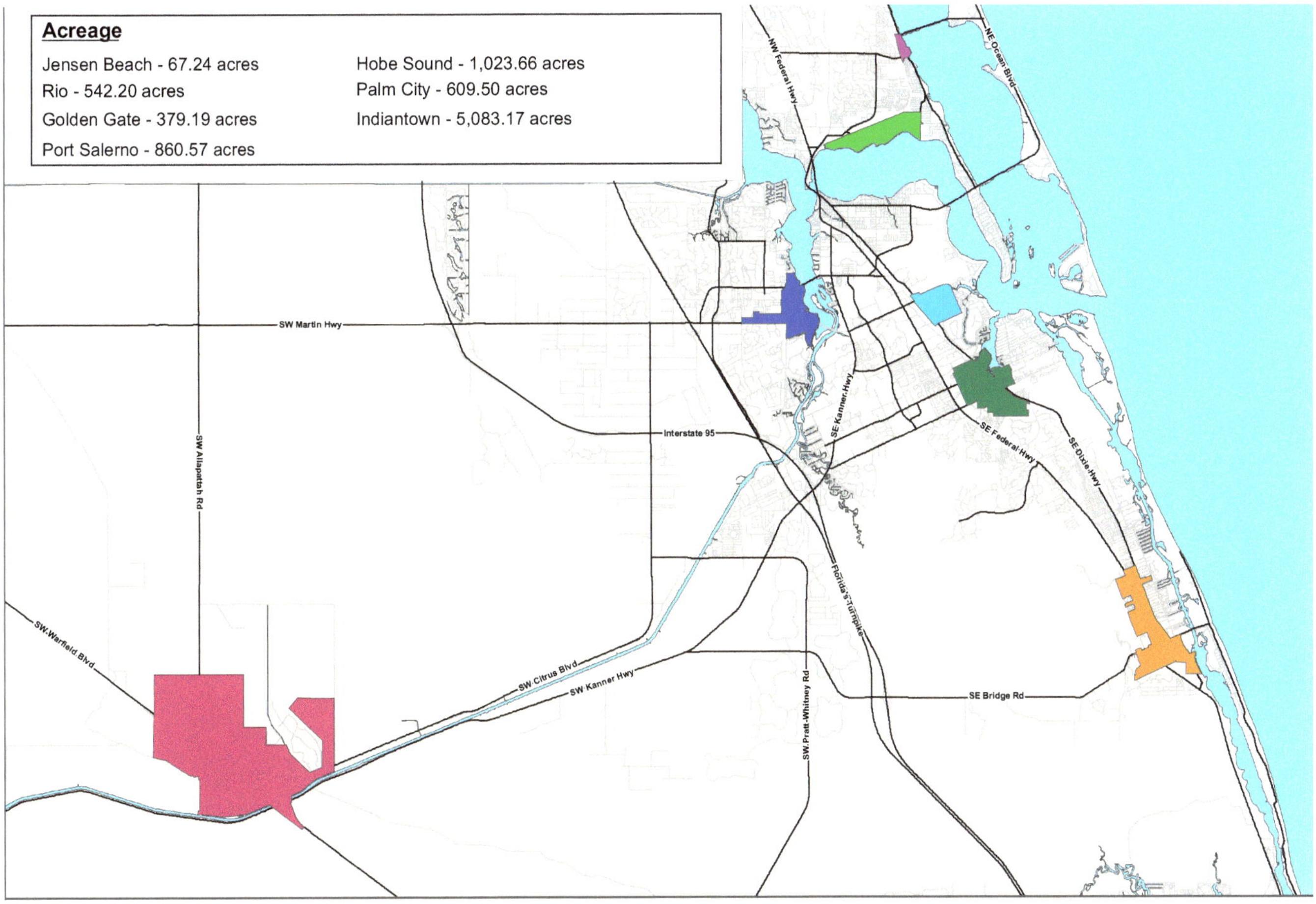
Acreage
Jensen Beach - 67.24 acres
Rio - 542.20 acres
Golden Gate - 379.19 acres
Port Salerno - 860.57 acres
Hobe Sound - 1,023.66 acres
Palm City - 609.50 acres
Indiantown - 5,083.17 acres
NW Federal Hwy
NE Ocean Blvd
SW Martin Hwy
SE Kanner Hwy
Interstate 95
SE Federal Hwy
SE Dixie Hwy
SW Allapattah Rd
Florida's Turnpike
SW Warfield Blvd
SW Citrus Blvd
SW Kanner Hwy
SW Pratt-Whitney Rd
SE Bridge Rd

COMMUNITY REDEVELOPMENT AREAS

Between 2000 and 2002, the Martin County Board of County Commissioners recognized the unfulfilled potential of seven established neighborhoods within the County and designated them as community redevelopment areas:

- Golden Gate
- Hobe Sound
- Indiantown
- Jensen Beach
- Old Palm City
- Port Salerno
- Rio

When combined, these community redevelopment areas make up 8,565.5 acres or just over 2.4% of the acreage within Martin County.

Each of the seven areas is diverse with characteristics ranging from coastal communities to rural agricultural centers. This diversity provides a wide variety of opportunities to live, work, play and invest.

Over the years the CRA has facilitated redevelopment via the adequate and efficient provision of infrastructure, housing and other community services. These investments help to preserve, promote, and improve the quality of life within the seven community redevelopment areas.

Area Summary

CRA Areas:
- Golden Gate
- Hobe Sound
- Indiantown
- Jensen Beach
- Old Palm City
- Port Salerno
- Rio

Plan Adoptions: 2001-2002

Total Area:
- 8,565.5 Acres
- 2.4% of Martin County

Recent Projects:
- Completed the development of Google 3D maps
- Analysis of the per acre taxable values
- Acquisition of blighted properties
- Redevelopment Technical Assistance
- Design review and permitting
- Drafting of the Community Oriented Code
- Development of a Business Training Program to support local microentrepreneurs .

Area Specific Special Designations:
- Neighborhood Stabilization Program (NSP) Target Area
- Mixed-Use Overlay
- Designated Florida Enterprise Zone
- Waterfront Florida Community

Google 3D Mapping

More than 350 million internet users have turned to Google Earth© and Google Mapping to better understand and navigate their world. They use these tools to observe their community from above, but also to consider a real-estate investment, to plan a travel itinerary, or to look at a cityscape from a new perspective. The Martin County Community Redevelopment Agency is set to be the first community on the Treasure Coast to undertake Google Earth 3D Mapping and utilize it as a tool for future planning within the community redevelopment areas.

In addition to utilizing Google Earth 3D modeling as a planning tool, this mapping technology increases the exposure of our local businesses on the web. Local businesses will have the ability to connect their business information and website to these maps. The Community Redevelopment Agency will initially begin with mapping business corridors within the Golden Gate, Hobe Sound and Port Salerno community redevelopment areas.

As the models were uploaded and accepted by Google, our communities began to see an increased visibility on the web. Our local Redevelopment Areas climbed on the search engine lists. Local business' contact information and locations became easier to find, which in turn generated online and foot traffic to these location.

Project Type:
- Mapping
- Marketing

Funding Source:
- Tax Increment Finance (TIF) $32,100

Status: Complete

Project Manager: Edward W. Erfurt

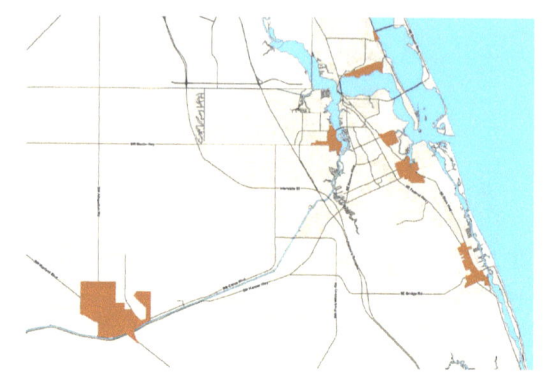

Property Appraisal Evaluation

The Community Redevelopment Agency annually maps the appraised property values in the redevelopment areas to evaluate the property tax implications of different development types and the return on investment for capital projects. Through simple math, the CRA is able to illustrate the total property value per acre throughout each redevelopment area. Over several years of this mapping, staff is able to reflect and compare the growth in these land values which provides real data for future investment and growth in the redevelopment areas.

There are several projects in the redevelopment areas that demonstrate a positive impact property values. In Port Salerno, the CRA assisted Habitat for Humanity in the development of seven affordable homes by extending water a sewer. Prior to the development in 2010, the land was appraised at $99,300. The CRA invested $65,000 in utility expansion and staff time in planning. Today, five of seven homes have been built. The total appraised value today is $457,720, which is a 460% increase in value. In addition, the adjacent properties have also increased in value.

Project Type:
- Analysis
- Forecasting

Funding Source:
- Staff Allocation

Status: On-going

Project Manager: Edward W. Erfurt

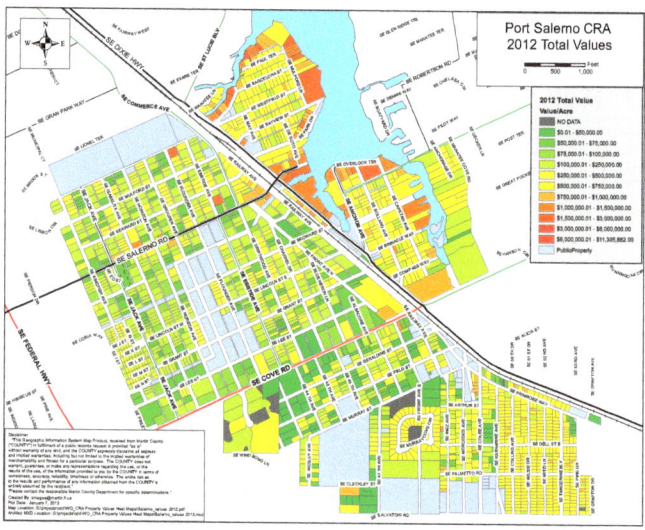

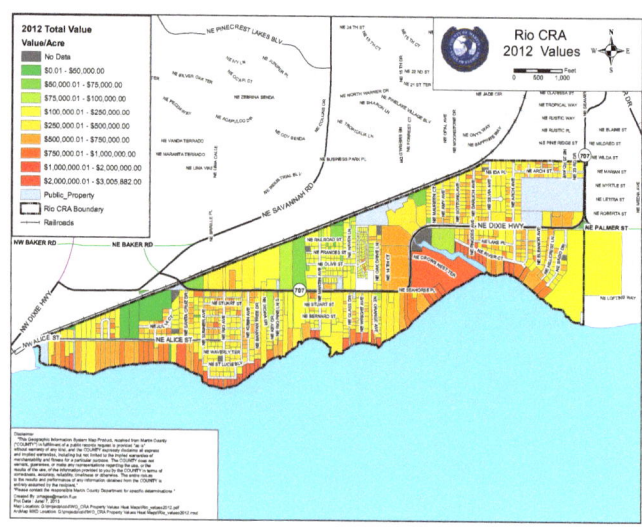

Property Acquisition

As contemplated in both, Florida Statutes and Countywide Community Redevelopment Plan, the Community Redevelopment Agency may acquire property within a slum or blighted area by purchase, lease, option, gift, grant, bequest, devise, or other voluntary method of acquisition to meet the goals and objectives of the Community Redevelopment Plan.

In FY13 the Community Redevelopment Agency coordinated with the Building's Department Code Enforcement Division and Engineering's Department Property Management Division, the acquisition of properties subject to multiple code enforcement fines and as part of roadway improvement projects..

The following are the properties owned by the Martin County CRA at the end of FY13. Staff are working towards a disposition program that will be presented to the Board of County Commissioners for approval.

Property Address	Redevelopment Area	Acreage
1195 NE Martin Street	Rio	0.1263
977 NE Dixie Highway	Rio	0.2836
16870 SW Charleston Street	Indiantown	1.0124
1310 NE Dixie Highway	Rio	0.1900
1150 NE Dixie Highway	Rio	0.2583

1150 NE Dixie

1195 NE Martin Street

1310 NE Dixie

1195 NE Martin Street

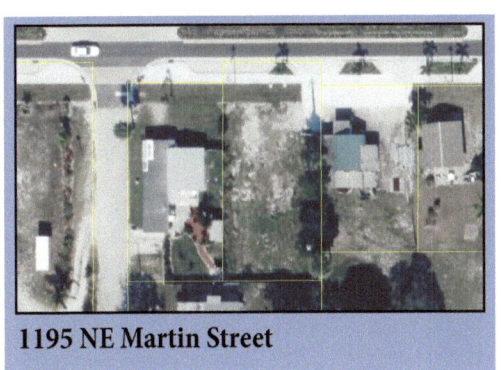
1195 NE Martin Street

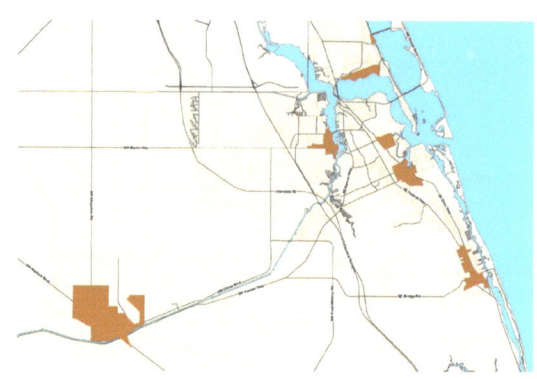

Redevelopment Technical Assistance

The mission of the Community Redevelopment Agency is to promote a distinctive community identity and vibrant local economy which is supported by the Community Redevelopment Plans and Overlay Land Development Regulations. To support future development that is consistent with the community vision, Community Development Staff engage property owners and development teams throughout the development process.

The Community Development Department Staff is composed of professionals with the education and experience in the fields of planning, architecture, and engineering, and a working institutional knowledge of Martin County's Comprehensive Plan, Land Development Regulations, and Permitting Processes. This experience provides a competitive advantage that attracts private investment in the CRA, while championing and promoting the community vision with each new development.

This process has resulted in numerous Minor Site Plan Applications being ready and approved for a Development Order in the first round of review and in less than 40 days. These results are attracting new investment and leading to an increased number of development applications and building permits in the CRA.

Project Type:
- Redevelopment
- Economic Development

Funding Source:
- Staff Allocation

Status: On-going

Project Manager: Edward W. Erfurt

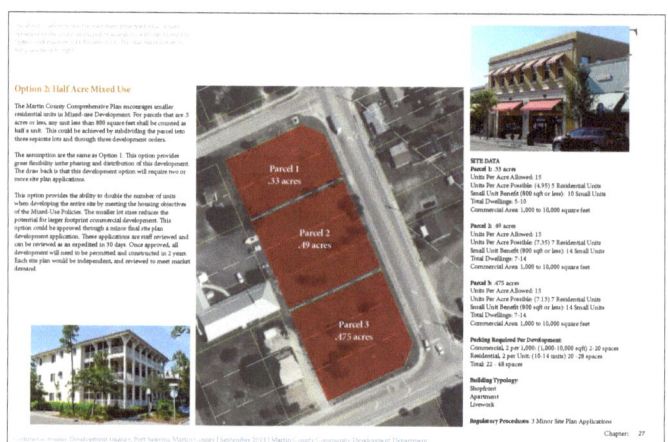

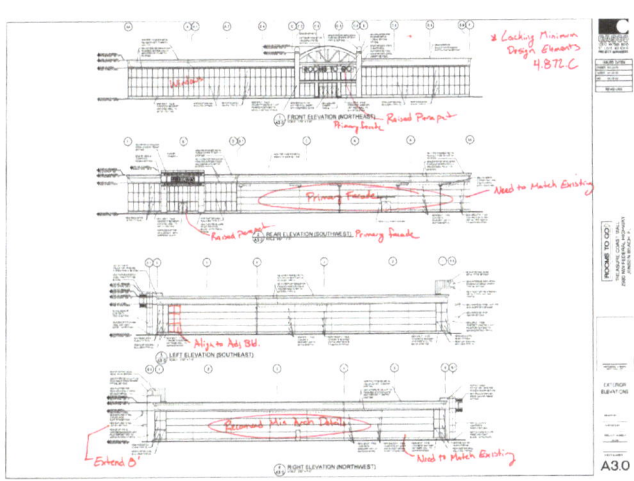

Design Review & Permitting

The Community Redevelopment Agency provides professional technical services to the public, the Martin County Growth Management Department, and the Martin County Building Department, to promote a distinctive community identity throughout the seven community redevelopment areas while supporting a vibrant local economy.

Staff provides technical support to property owners within the CRA boundaries by familiarizing owners with development requirements and illustrating how regulations may be applied to their specific site. This hands-on approach involves proactively meeting with the developer of a site to understand their desires and connect them to the community's vision. Once an applicant begins the formal development process, staff serves as an advocate for the project and assists in moving the application through required review in an expeditious manner.

Staff also meets with professionals in the field of architecture, construction, and real estate to educate and promote redevelopment and investment within the redevelopment areas.

As a member of the Martin County's Development Review Team, staff participates in the permit review of development and building applications within the CRA. Staff is able to act as voice for residents through these permits. In addition, the Urban Designer reviews all commercial development applications Countywide.

In FY2013 there were a total of 935 building permits issued in the CRA. This accounts for 9% of the total building permits in Martin County with a valuation of $12.4 million dollars. This is a 10% increase in the number of permits in private investment in the CRA from the previous year.

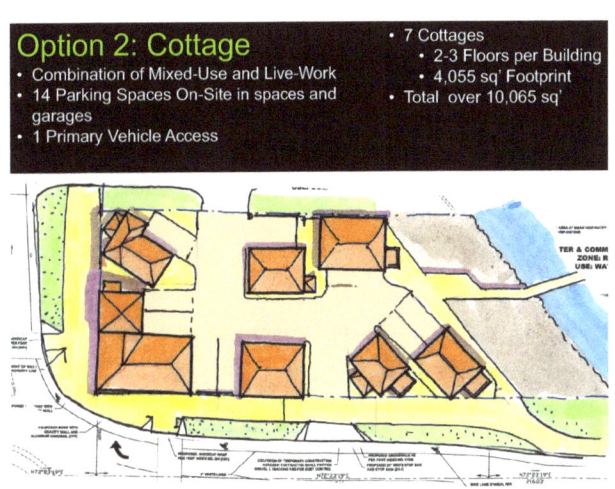

Option 2: Cottage
- Combination of Mixed-Use and Live-Work
- 14 Parking Spaces On-Site in spaces and garages
- 1 Primary Vehicle Access
- 7 Cottages
- 2-3 Floors per Building
- 4,055 sq' Footprint
- Total over 10,065 sq'

Project Type:
- Redevelopment
- Urban Design Review
- Permitting

Funding Source:
- Staff Allocation

Status: On-going

Project Manager: Edward W. Erfurt

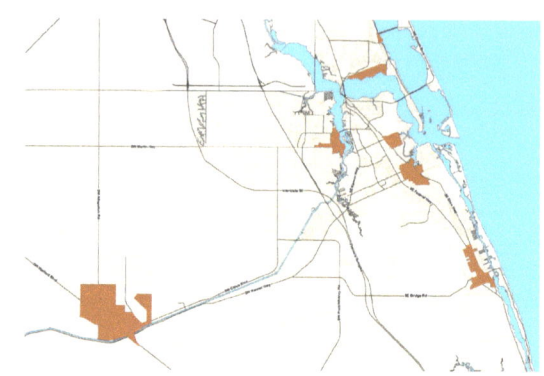

Community Oriented Code

Currently the community redevelopment areas consist of eight (8) different Land Development Regulations, five (5) different Architectural Design Requirements, and two (2) separate parking studies. In addition to these regulations, new code provisions have been added to the Martin County Land Development Regulations.

These governing regulations were developed independently over several years by various consultant teams. As a result, there is often inconsistency in the language and content of these regulations, resulting in frustration, confusion, and a complicated development review and permitting process.

In an effort to streamline the development process the CRA is currently working with a qualified consultant to establish a unifying visually based code for all seven community redevelopment areas.

In collaboration with the community and the Growth Management Department, staff has outlined all of the performance standards currently regulated in all of the existing codes, and identified where duplication can be eliminated. Staff is working with Growth Management, Engineering, and the Legal Department, to integrate Parking, Roadway, Landscaping, and Signage requirements in the code. These proposed revisions will be shared with the Public and presented to the Board of County Commissions in 2014 for adoption.

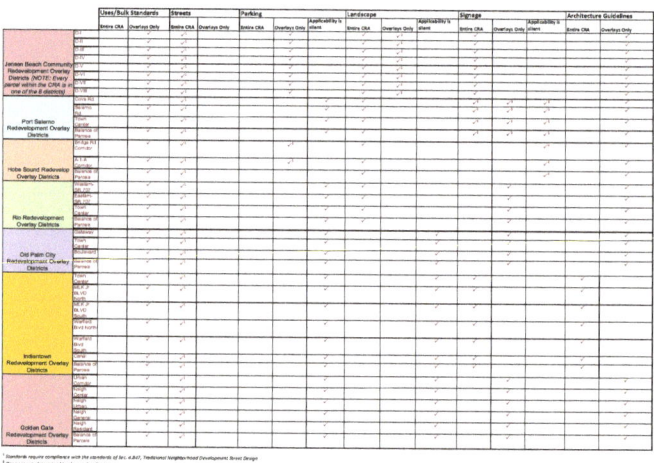

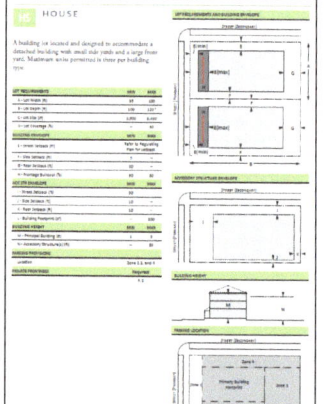

Project Type:
- Zoning and Community

Planning Funding Source:
- Tax Increment Finance $198,000

Status: In progress

Project Manager:
Nakeischea Smith, AICP
Edward W. Erfurt

Martin County Board of County Commissioners
Your County, Your Community

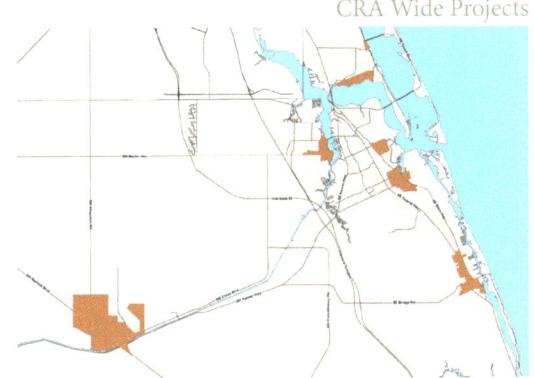

Business Training Program (Support for Local Microentrepreneurs)

The Community Redevelopment Agency is working on the proposal of a Business Training Program to promote the creation of new Microenterprises and support the growth of existing ones. This Program will provide future entrepreneurs, microenterprise owners and small business owners with valuable business training and key resources, essential to start, manage and grow a successful business.

The purpose of the training is to prepare potential entrepreneurs, business owners and employees in the most needed and useful areas of business fundamentals to enhance their skills so they can not only overcome challenging situations but also be prepared to follow the path to growth and success. This entrepreneurship education will also build confidence, strengthen the entrepreneurial mindset, motivate progress and inspire action.

In FY13, the Community Development Department proposed a partnership with Indian River State College's Dan K. Richardson Entrepreneurship Development Institute (EDI) to set up the details of the program.

Community Development Staff is currently working with The Corporate Training Institute (CCTI), the Small Business Development Center (SBDC), and Indian River State College (IRSC) Virtual Incubator staff on the curricula.

Project Type:
- Economic Development

Funding Source:
- Staff Allocation
- Tax Increment Finance (TIF)

Status: Proposed

Project Manager: Nancy Johnsom

Golden Gate

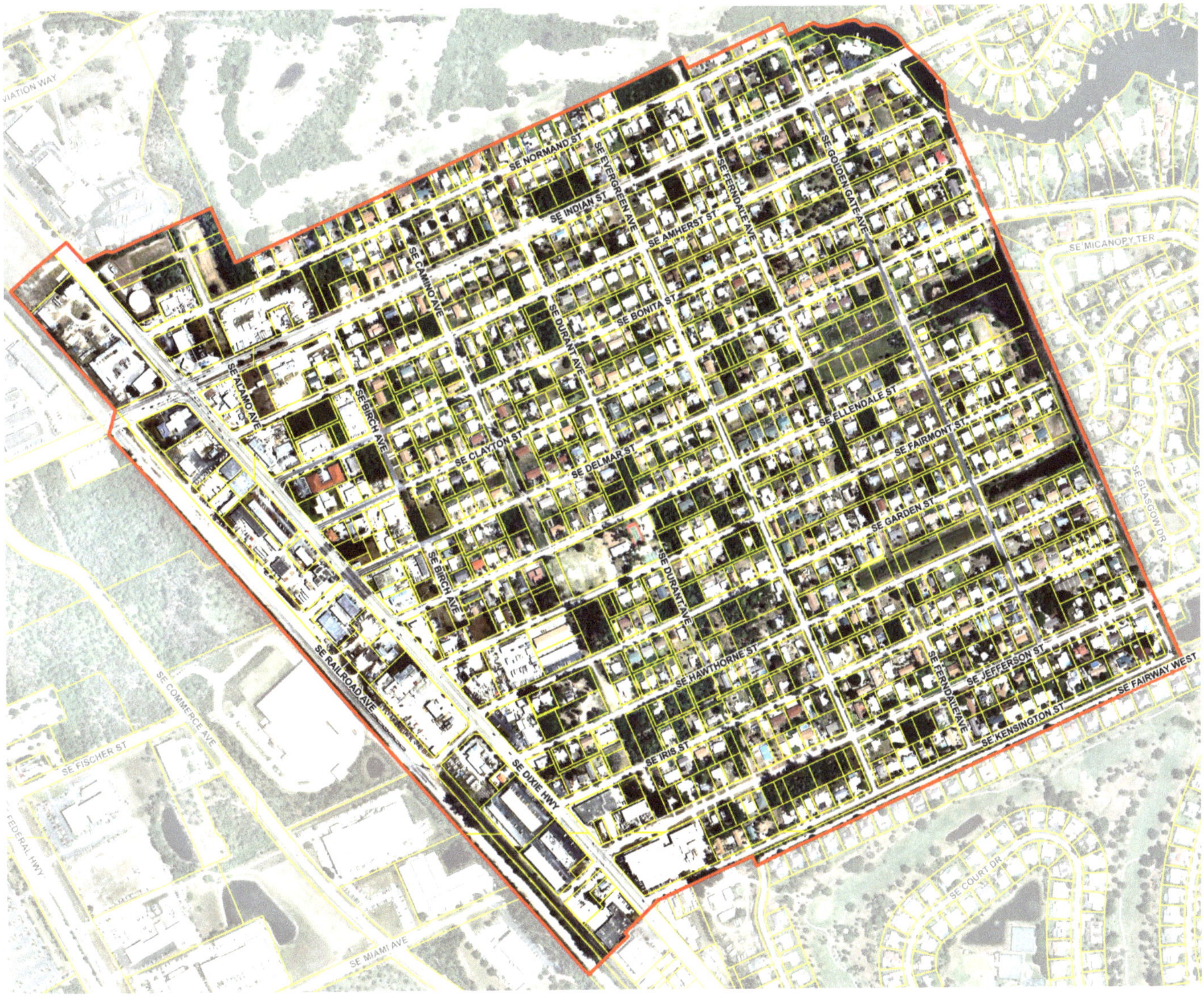

GOLDEN GATE The historic Community was platted in 1925 by the Golden Gate Development Company. The community is located adjacent to Witham Field airport, just over two miles south of the City of Stuart and bounded by the Florida East Coast Railroad.

Historically, Golden Gate was intended to become a fashionable resort area offering the best natural amenities in Florida. Its position on the St. Lucie River, which leads to the St. Lucie Inlet and the Atlantic Ocean, made it an ideal location for a port city.

The original buildings were built in the Mediterranean Revival and Spanish Mission styles. One original commercial building and fourteen original houses remain in the neighborhood today.

With an ideal location within the heart of the Treasure Coast, residential and commercial investment opportunities abound.

The community vision for Golden Gate is to flourish both economically and culturally. The CRA and the County are working on providing basic infrastructure improvements, such as pedestrian accommodation, storm water management and sewer expansion to make this vision a reality.

Area Summary

CRA Area: Golden Gate
Plan Adoption: September 2002
Total Area: 379 Acres

Area Highlights:
- Proximity to Witham Field Airport
- Access to FEC Rail

Recent Projects:
- Railroad Avenue Commercial Revitalization Project

Special Designations:
- Neighborhood Stabilization Program (NSP) Target Area

Railroad Avenue
Commercial Revitalization Project

The Railroad Avenue Commercial Revitalization project was identified by Golden Gate residents as a targeted area for redevelopment both in the 2002 Golden Gate Redevelopment Plan and the 2010 Neighborhood Opportunity Workshop.

This commercial corridor consists of a dirt roadway which will be reconstructed utilizing Tax Increment Financing and a $700,000 Community Development Block Grant made possible by the Florida Department of Economic Opportunity.

Streetscape improvements will include paving, installation of curbing and sidewalks, landscape, signage, on-street parking, and drainage facilities. The project will provide formalized access to businesses along the corridor, improve safety, and eliminate encroachments onto the Martin County Right of Way and the Federal East Coast Railway Right of Way.

Project construction will begin in December 2012 and is expected to continue through Fall of 2013.

Project Type: Mixed-Use
Funding Source:
- Community Development Block Grant $700,000
- TMDL Grant $188,500
- Tax Increment Finance (TIF) $84,967
- Utilities Department $25,578

Status:
- Under Construction

Project Manager: Nakeischea Smith, AICP

Hobe Sound

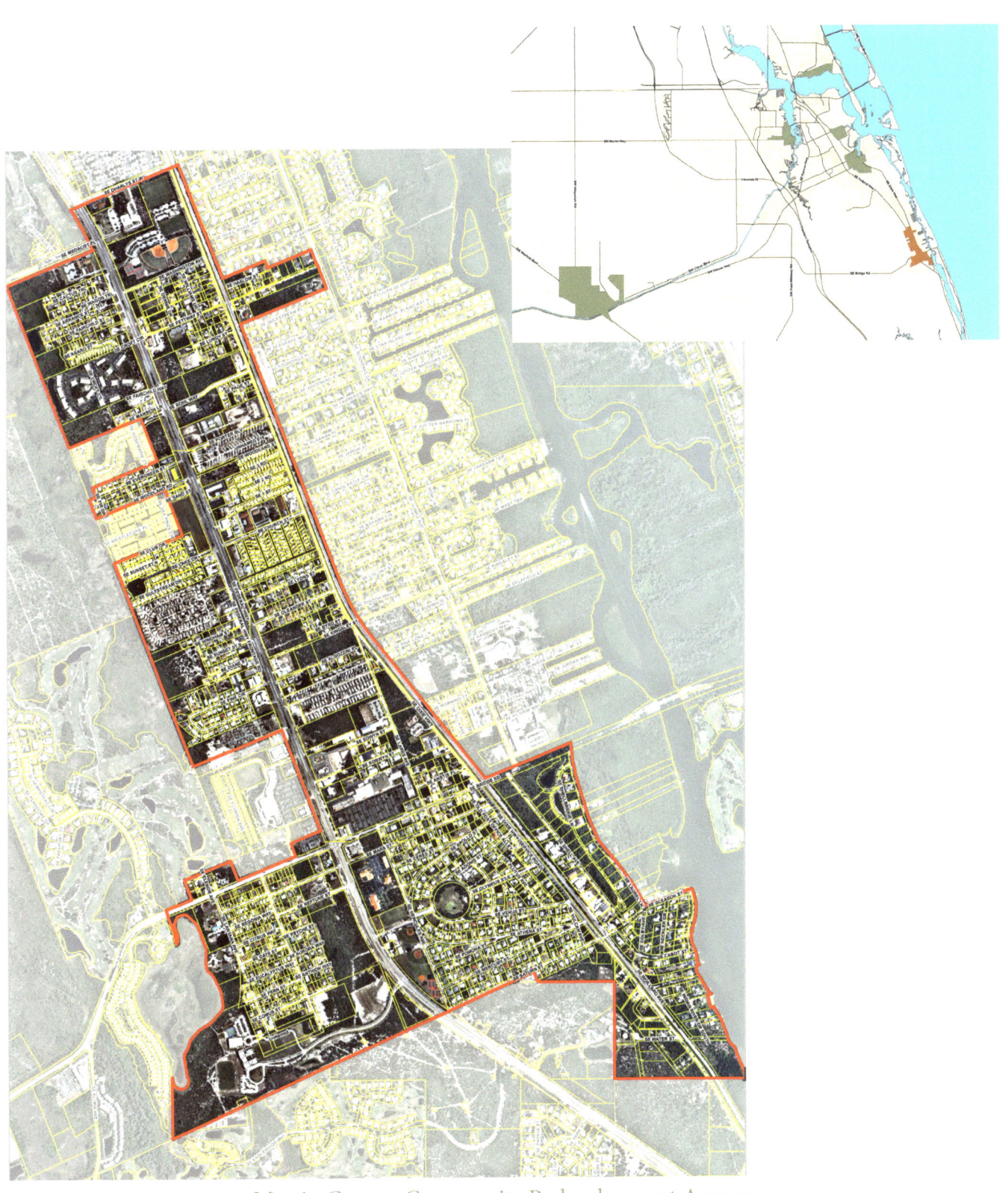

HOBE SOUND community redevelopment area extends along the east and west sides of US-1 from Osprey Road to Dharyls Street. It also includes the area bounded by Bridge Road to the north, Lantana Avenue and Banner Lake to the west, the Intracoastal Waterway to the east and the Eaglewood Golf Course and US-1 to the south.

The predominant land use within the redevelopment area is residential. These residential areas represent noteworthy examples of traditional neighborhood development patterns.

The "small-town" character and extensive environmental amenities that are characteristic of Hobe Sound make the community an attractive location.

The community desires to retain and reinforce a small town, village like setting within Hobe sound. CRA investment in infrastructure such as sewer systems and the adoption of design regulations serve to promote and encourage compatible and appropriate redevelopment in keeping with the community vision.

Area Summary

CRA Area: Hobe Sound
Plan Adoption: December 2000
Total Area: 1,024 Acres

Area Highlights:
- Southern Gateway into Martin County from Jupiter Island and Palm Beach
- Access to FEC Rail

Recent Projects:
- Bridge Road Main Street

Special Designations:
- Mixed-Use Overlay

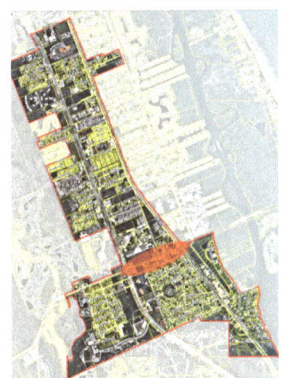

Bridge Road Main Street

Plans to enhance Bridge Road between US-1 and Dixie Highway officially began in 2000 with the establishment of the Hobe Sound Redevelopment Plan. Precursor goals for the corridor were identified as early as 1994. Bridge Road was highlighted as the #1 focus area in the 2010 NOW Visioning community report. The vision for Bridge Road is that of a sustainable neighborhood "Main Street" setting that will support a vibrant downtown for all. Objectives of the Bridge Road project include increasing the amount of on-street parking, improving vehicular and pedestrian safety, undergrounding overhead utilities, improving drainage, reducing speeds, and promoting walkability through sidewalk additions and landscape enhancements.

Staff has worked closely with the Hobe Sound Neighborhood Advisory Committee (NAC) and the community on the corridor design since early 2011. Staff has also engaged with businesses owners and property owners along Bridge Road by hosting open houses and scheduling one-on-one meetings. Participation by the NAC, residents, business owners and property owners ensures the design will meet the individual needs of each business along the corridor and align with the vision as outlined in the Hobe Sound Redevelopment Plan.

Engineering drawings are currently being drafted, accounting for the needs of the property owners and businesses along Bridge Road.

The Martin County Board of County Commissioners have approved the acceptance of any right of way needed to complete the project. Staff is coordinating with property owners and Martin County's Property Management department to accept additional right of way needed to make the project a reality.

Project Type:
- "Complete Streets"
- Innovative Stormwater Management
- Utility Undergrounding
- Roadway Reconstruction

Proposed Funding Source:
- Tax Increment Financing (TIF)
- Grants

Status: In Design

Project Manager: Nakeischea Smith, AICP

Indiantown

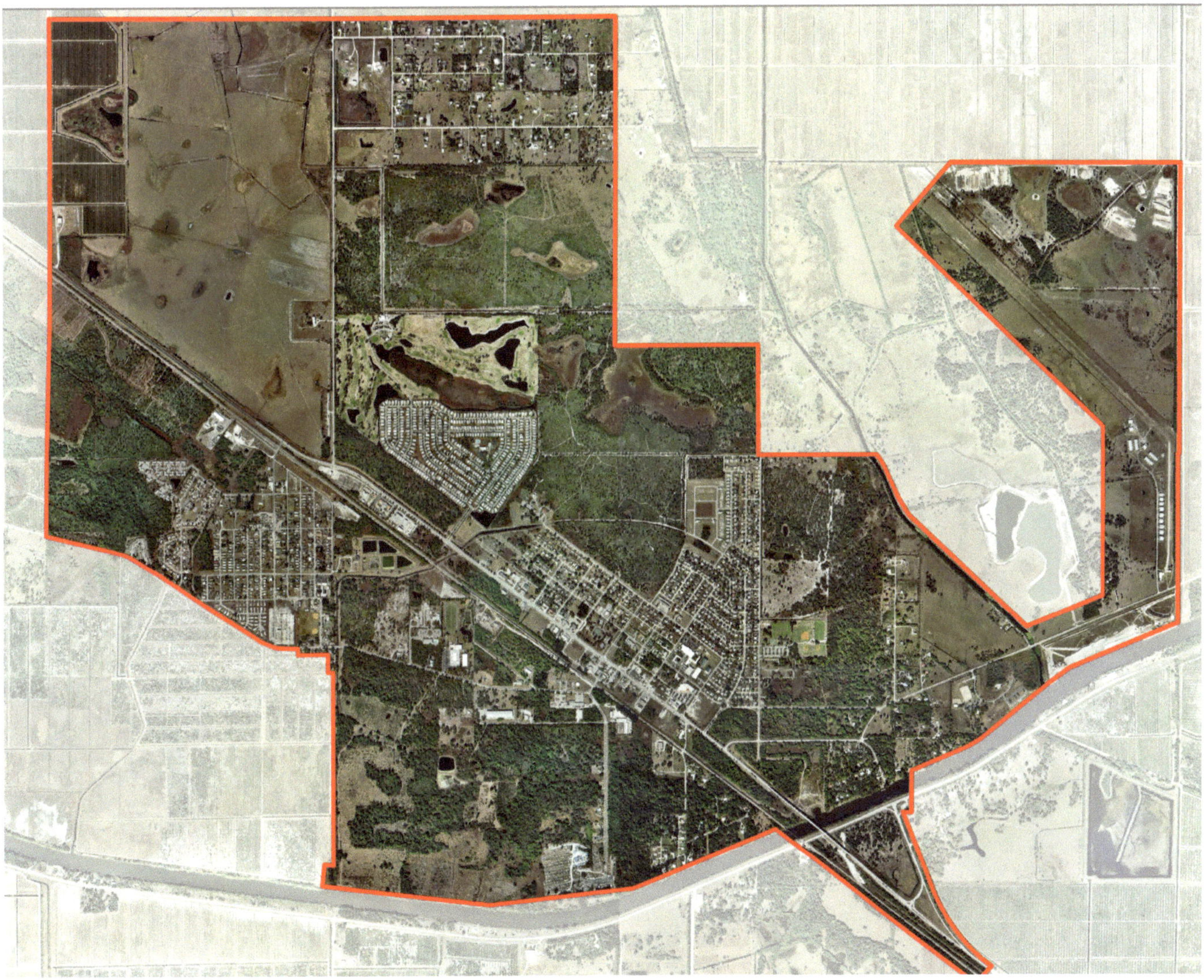

INDIANTOWN is a small, quiet town just outside the fast paced, rapidly growing South Florida metropolitan area. It is an unincorporated part of Martin County, about 15 miles west of Stuart, and about 8 miles north of the Palm Beach County line, surrounded by citrus groves and cattle ranches. Home to just under 7,000 residents, Indiantown is a culturally and ethnically diverse community, surrounded by a rural greenbelt consisting mainly of agriculture. Its location, history, demographics and residents make it unique.

Indiantown consists of a mix of residential housing and neighborhoods which include a significant senior population who has chosen to retire there.

The community envisions Indiantown as an ethnically diverse, clean, safe, and friendly small town with rural character and feel. The community wants the town to be economically thriving and balanced with an industrial, corporate, and commercial base providing good jobs, services, and products available for all its residents.

Area Summary

CRA Area: Indiantown
Plan Adoption: December 2002
Total Area: 5,083 Acres

Area Highlights:
- Largest rural community within Martin County with an economic base served by agricultural industries and the FPL Next Generation Solar Energy Center
- Strong transportation infrastructure that includes State Road 710, CSX Railway, the C-44 Canal, and Indiantown Airport which boasts the east coast longest grass landing strip

Recent Projects:
- Vertical Development at Carter Park

Special Designations:
- Designated Florida Enterprise Zone

McDonalds/Dollar General

The Indiantown McDonalds/Dollar General project received a development order in 2012, and is the first new commercial development application approved within Indiantown in over 20 years.

In late spring 2013, construction began, and the McDonalds and Dollar General opened their doors in late summer. This development created over 80 new permanent jobs in Indiantown where the unemployment rate has been 12.7 percent.

The 2013 tax rolls generated by the Martin County Property Appraiser only reflect the horizontal site improvements. These records show a 375 percent increase in land value from the previous year and a 175 percent increase in property value from the establishment of the CRA. The vertical improvements of over $1.5 million will be reflected in the 2014 taxable value, and will add to the tax base in Indiantown.

Project Type: Private Development
Funding Source:
- Staff Allocation
- Private Investment

Status: Approved Development Order
Project Manager: Edward W. Erfurt

Carter Park

Carter Park began to become a physical reality in 2012 with the completed development order and plat for Carter Park. In 2013, the site construction was completed, and project partners began vertical construction.

The center of the Carter Park neighborhood is a one acre stormwater pond that treats 256 acres of run-off from existing development. As required by The Maximum Daily Load (TMDL) Grant, the County monitored the stormwater quality as a result of this project. The constructed treatment train system is removing 78% of Total Suspended Solids (TSS), 86% of Total Nitrogen (TN), and 43% of Total Phosphorous (TP) . Other pollutants/nutrients including Total Kjeldahl Nitrogen (TKN) and nitrate/nitrite have removal efficiencies of 59% and orthophosphate a removal efficiency of 54%.

Habitat for Humanity built and dedicated four affordable and green homes in Carter Park, and is preparing work for four additional homes. In addition to fulfilling the need for quality affordable housing, the Martin County Property Appraiser is reporting an increase in taxable value for these properties. The tax bills for the first two homes exceed the previous tax bill for the entire pre-development 12 acre site. As additional families move into this community, the tax revenue will continue to grow.

The Boys and Girls Club started construction of the new 22,000 square foot Club which should open in April 2014. The County is working with the Boys and Girls Club on the implementation of the final right of way improvements adjacent to the Club. In addition, Martin County Transit is exploring a new transit stop in front of the Club.

Project Type:
- Affordable Housing Development
- Innovative Stormwater Management
- Parks and recreation

Funding Source:
- FDEP TMDL Grant $600,000
- Tax Increment Financing (TIF) $1.5 million
- Western 1 District MSTU $100,000
- Road MSTU Fund $300,000

Status:
- Complete
- Private Development Underway

Project Manager: Edward W. Erfurt

Martin County Board of County Commissioners
Your County, Your Community

Martin County Community Redevelopment Agency
Redevelopment in Action

Jensen Beach

JENSEN BEACH is a historic riverfront/ocean side resort community located in northern Martin County that is bounded by the Indian River Lagoon, and the Florida East Coast Railway. Proximity to Hutchinson Island, the Atlantic Beaches and the Indian River Lagoon, attract tourists and visitors which drives this community's economy. Redevelopment activities began for Jensen Beach as early as 1986.

The CRA district is distinctively defined on the south by the Town of Ocean Breeze Park, which is an incorporated mobile home park; and on the west by the FEC Railroad. The eastern boundary is the Indian River while the northern boundary is the Jensen Beach causeway. Jensen Beach encompasses approximately 65 acres, with a collection of small, popular locally owned business and art galleries. Despite its relatively small size, Jensen Beach still has over 50% of its area vacant and ready for redevelopment.

The Indian River provides the obvious scenic amenity, as well as fishing, boating and water related opportunities. The railroad has the potential to provide future passenger traffic for both tourism and commuting.

Jensen Beach's unique history, small cottage businesses, dedicated residents, and its prime location on the Indian River, are the community's most significant assets. The goal of the Jensen Beach CRA is to enhance the area's character which includes an eclectic, pedestrian-friendly community. The CRA envisions a continuation of the 'casual' Jensen Beach atmosphere which emphasizes a mix of uses, an active street life, Florida vernacular architecture, enhanced landscaping, and coordinated signage.

Area Summary

CRA Area: Jensen Beach
Plan Adoption: September 2002
Total Area: 67

Area Highlights:
- Waterfront community with an existing marina and commercial docks
- Gateway to Hutchinson Island
- FEC Rail crossing and access

Recent Projects:
- Enhancements to Indian River Drive

Special Designations:
- Jensen Beach Community Redevelopment Area

Indian River Drive Complete Street

The Community Development Department is collaborating with Martin County Engineering Department to improve Indian River Drive in Jensen Beach. These improvements include, on-street parking, wide sidewalks, landscaping, and stormwater enhancements as outlined in the Jensen Beach Community Redevelopment Plan.

Planned improvements are based on a modular design that facilitates incremental redevelopment along this riverfront corridor. This innovative approach was first implemented in 2010, when the County received a grant to add stormwater treatment to the roadway. This provided the funding for the east side of the road to be constructed.

Staff is working with several property owners adjacent to Indian River Drive to acquire the right of way needed on the west side of the road to implement the complete roadway section as outlined in the community vision.

Project Type:
- Streetscape enhancements

Proposed Funding Source:
- TIF
- 707 Repaving Funds

Status:
- Preliminary Design and Planning

Project Manager: Edward W. Erfurt

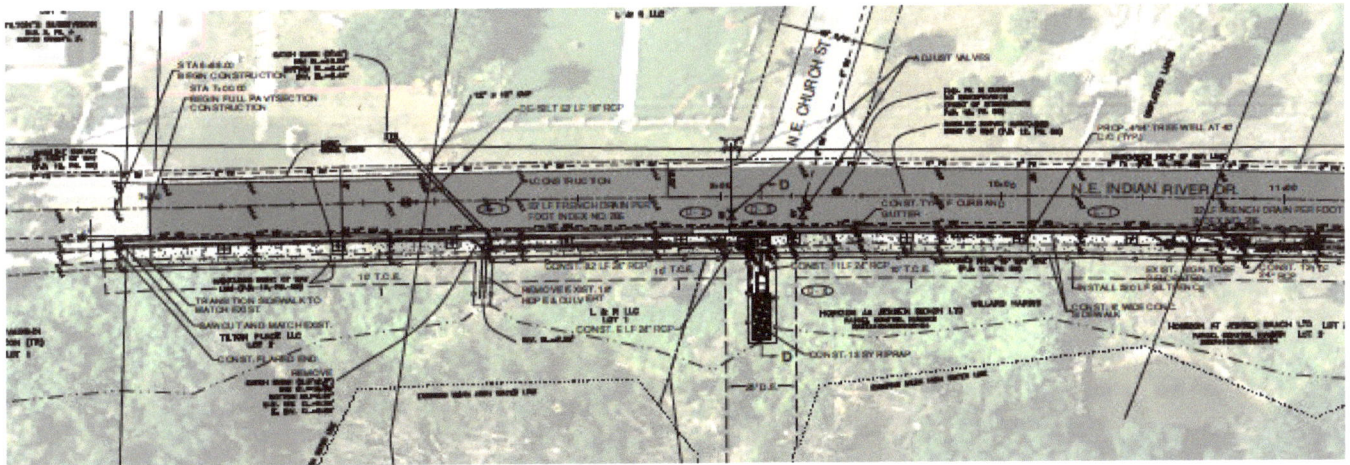

Old Palm City

OLD PALM CITY is located between Martin Downs and Martin Highway along the south fork of the St. Lucie River.

Old Palm City is an interconnected community that continues to exhibit a traditional small town/village setting. Homes are close together and most front on quiet residential streets that invite social interaction and form the foundation for a pleasant, quality living environment.

Schools, parks and small businesses are within walking distance of most of the residents within the redevelopment area. This presents an opportunity to foster positive growth and development.

The CRA and the County are working on providing basic infrastructure improvements, such as pedestrian accommodation, stormwater management and sewer expansion, to provide a competitive edge for job creation and investment in the CRA, specifically along Mapp Road.

Area Summary

CRA Area: Old Palm City
Plan Adoption: April 2002
Total Area: 610 Acres

Area Highlights:
- Waterfront Community
- Home to Several Targeted Businesses

Recent Projects:
- Planning for Improvements on Mapp Road
- Construction of the Indian Street Bridge

Special Designations:
- Old Palm City Community Redevelopment Area

Mapp Road Town Center Design

Improvements for Mapp Road as outlined in the 2003 Old Palm City Redevelopment Plan included a desire for an old-fashioned Main Street, on-street parking, and a safe, well-connected corridor that allowed for various modes of transportation including walking and biking.

The CRA began in earnest in 2008 to make this project a reality. Engineering design drawings were prepared that included parallel parking, landscaped medians, and construction of a stormwater management system capable of handling future improvements.

In 2010, the design was updated utilizing more innovative strategies such as head out angled parking to replace parallel parking stalls, and rain gardens to better incorporate best stormwater management practices and improve environmental health. Center medians were removed as a cost saving measure and a modular design approach was introduced that did not require the entire roadway to be constructed all at once.

Through a series of public workshops led by staff in 2012, the community voiced their preference for a simpler design that would allow for construction of the entire corridor, rather than a modular approach.

The CRA expects to begin retooling and reprioritizing components of the design in 2013 in keeping with the community's desire. With $1.3 million available in TIF for construction, the CRA will seek a design that can be implemented for the entire corridor and which aligns with the available TIF dollars.

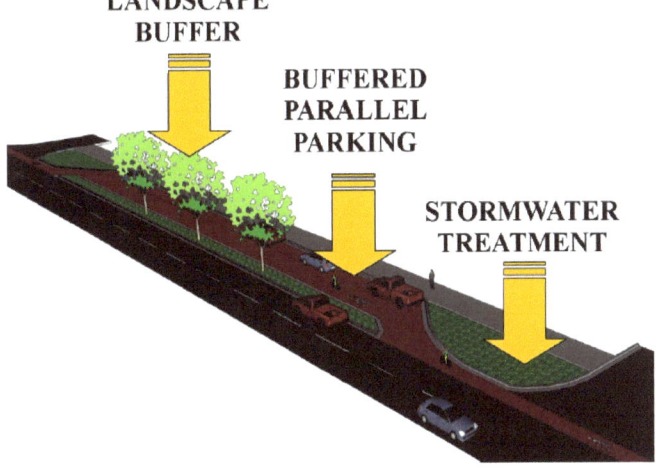

LANDSCAPE BUFFER

BUFFERED PARALLEL PARKING

STORMWATER TREATMENT

Project Type:
- Complete Streets
- Innovative Stormwater Management

Funding Source:
- Tax Increment Financing (TIF)

Status:
- Initial design complete, retooling in progress

Project Manager: Erik Ferguson

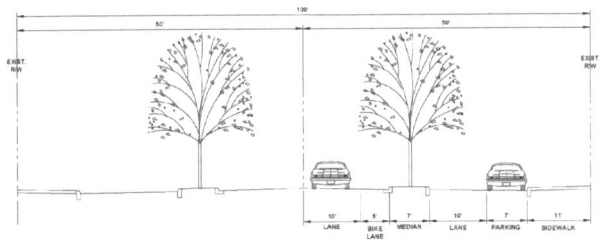

MAPP ROAD Blvd. Traditional Bike Lane Concept

Port Salerno

PORT SALERNO is defined by the Manatee Pocket, which extends from the Port Salerno to the St. Lucie Inlet and is fed by several creeks. The St. Lucie Inlet and Manatee Pocket provide an ideal harbor for fisherman working the Atlantic Ocean, and is the primary reason Port Salerno was originally settled.

Port Salerno has a strong commercial core connected to the waterfront on A1A, and two commercial corridors along Salerno and Cove Roads. Adjacent to these commercial centers are dense residential neighborhoods.

Today, Port Salerno is influenced by a shifting economy that replaced the traditional fishing industry with resort and recreational fishing. The port, with access to the Atlantic Ocean, continues to be an attractive economic amenity as boating manufacturing, repair and sales, have located in Port Salerno.

Waterfront access continues to be an attraction as recreational boaters rely on the services of the marine industries, and visitors enjoy the ever-growing public waterfront access.

The Port Salerno redevelopment area is bounded by Cove Road on the south; St. Lucie River and A1A to the east.

Area Summary

CRA Area: Port Salerno
Plan Adoption: May 2000
Total Area: 861 Acres

Area Highlights:
- Designated Florida waterfront community with residents and visitors enjoying the ever-increasing public waterfront access
- Economic base served largely by commercial and recreational fishing industry, in addition to boat manufacturing, repair and sales.

Recent Projects:
- Micro Action Plans for the Manatee Creek Neighborhood

Special Designations:
- Waterfront Florida Community

Micro Action Plan (MAP): Manatee Creek

The Manatee Creek Micro Action Plan (MAP) outlines potential projects throughout the Manatee Creek neighborhood which includes sidewalk connections, gateway signage, ditch cleanup, addition of landscaping, community park improvements to include perimeter fencing, and safety improvements such as street lighting and cleanup of brush and ditches.

At their August 20, 2013 BOCC meeting, the Board adopted the resolution modifying the Port Salerno Community Redevelopment Plan to Incorporate the Manatee Creek MAP and allocated $10,000 from Port Salerno Tax Increment Finance (TIF) fund to assist in its implementation.

Project Type:
- Community Outreach
- Master Planning

Funding Source:
- Community Development Staff Time
- Tax Increment Financing (TIF) $5,000

Status:
- Adopted
- Implementing first recommendations

Project Manager: Erik Ferguson

Rio

RIO is bounded by Sewall's Point and Jensen Beach on the east, FEC Railway and Arch Street on the north, the City of Stuart on the west and the St. Lucie River to the south.
Rio is a waterfront community with both single family residential, multi-family units and commercial uses. Many of the commercial properties in Rio are small, individually owned and operated businesses.

Rio has the potential to become one of the most desirable places to live in Martin County due to its coastal location, energetic civic volunteers, historic architecture and colorful history.

The Rio CRA seeks to preserve Rio's history while making necessary improvements that will enhance Rio's future.

Area Summary

CRA Area: Rio
Plan Adoption: April 2001
Total Area: 542 Acres

Area Highlights:
- Waterfront community with two existing marinas
- Wide economic base with a mix of commercial and industrial land uses and a private rail spur

Projects:
- Resurfacing along 707 in Eastern Rio
- Development of the Rio Placemaking Plan
- Rhodes Avenue Gateway Enhancements
- Rio Porches Public Private Partnership

Special Designations:
- Neighborhood Stabilization Program (NSP) Target Area

Rhodes Avenue Gateway

The Rhodes Avenue Gateway Project was driven by community residents who desired a more visually appealing entrance to their neighborhood that would serve as a buffer between the commercial and residential areas.

Staff worked closely with adjacent residents and the Rio Neighborhood Advisory Committee to select a plant palette for the site which includes sable palms, slash pine, silver palmetto, wax myrtle, dune sunflower, dwarf fakahatchee grass and limestone caprock.

The project was installed in May 2013.

Project Type:
- Gateway Enhancement

Funding Source:
- Tax Increment Financing (TIF) $8,000

Status: Completed

Project Manager: Nakeischea Smith, AICP

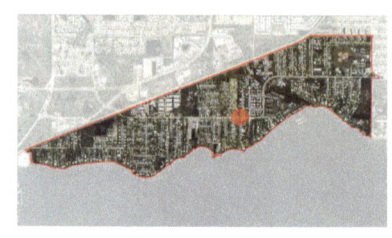

Rio Porches

Rio Porches is the former site of a deteriorated multiunit housing site within the Rio Town Center known as the Rainbow Cottages.

In late 2011, the property was purchased via auction. Upon purchase, the new owners expressed an interest in partnering with the CRA to redevelop the site in a manner reflective of the community vision.

Through this partnership, the CRA assisted with demolition of the dilapidated structures, and successfully negotiated a donation of additional right-of-way along the CR-707 frontage. This facilitated the extension of the CR-707 Roadway Retrofit project to the east.

The development is pending final site plan approval from the Growth Management Department, which will include two Live-Work Units, six one bedroom cottages, and will extend utility service south on Orange Avenue. Construction is scheduled to begin in the first quarter of 2014.

Project Type:
- Mixed Use Redevelopment
- Infill Housing

Funding Source:
- Private Investment
- Tax Increment Financing (TIF) $75,000

Status: Final Site Plan Pending Approval
Project Manager: Edward W. Erfurt